BAHRAIN: HUMAN RIGHTS

EXECUTIVE SUMMARY

Bahrain is a constitutional monarchy. King Hamad Bin Isa al-Khalifa, the head of state, appoints the cabinet consisting of 29 ministers; 13 of those ministers, excluding the deputy prime ministers, are members of the Sunni al-Khalifa ruling family. The parliament consists of an appointed upper house, the Shura (Consultative) Council, and an elected Council of Representatives. Approximately 17 percent of eligible voters participated in parliamentary by-elections for 18 seats vacated by the political opposition societies in September 2011. Independent human rights organizations did not consider the by-elections free and fair. In May 2012 the king ratified constitutional amendments broadening the powers of the elected chamber of parliament. Authorities maintained effective control over the security forces. Security forces committed human rights abuses.

The most serious human rights problems included citizens' inability to change their government peacefully; arrest and detention of protesters on vague charges, in some cases leading to their torture in detention; and lack of due process in trials of political and human rights activists, medical personnel, teachers, and students, with some trials resulting in harsh sentences.

Other significant human rights problems included arbitrary deprivation of life; lack of consistent accountability for security officers accused of committing human rights violations; arrest of individuals on charges relating to freedom of expression; reported violations of privacy; and restrictions on civil liberties, including freedom of speech, press, assembly, association, and some religious practices. The government at times imposed and enforced travel bans on political activists in conjunction with arrest charges. The government maintained the revocation of citizenship for 31 individuals and issued a decree regulating communications between political societies and foreign entities, which had not been enforced by year's end. Discrimination continued against the Shia population, as did discrimination on the basis of gender, religion, and nationality. There were reports of domestic violence against women and children. Trafficking in persons and restrictions on the rights of foreign workers continued to be significant problems.

Beginning in 2011 the country experienced a sustained period of unrest including mass protests calling for political reform. In 2011, 52 persons died in incidents linked to the unrest, and hundreds more were injured or arrested. The government prosecuted and sentenced some police personnel implicated in abuses committed during the year and dating back to 2011; however, authorities had not completed legal proceedings against security personnel, and it was unclear if security personnel were held in jail. Authorities reported that accused police officers were held in a special jail, apart from other detainees. The government took some steps to address the "culture of impunity," which the 2011 Bahrain Independent Commission of Inquiry (BICI) report identified, including establishing the Ministry of Interior's Ombudsman's Office and a Special Investigative Unit (SIU) in the Public Prosecutor's Office, reconstructing mosques destroyed during the 2011 unrest, re-instating nearly all dismissed workers, and acquitting medical personnel accused of crimes during the 2011 unrest. Additionally, in February the king relaunched the National Dialogue, which served as a forum for the government, legislature, and political societies to discuss a political solution. Following the arrest of senior al-Wifaq leader Khalil Marzooq, the opposition societies announced on September 18 they were suspending their participation in the dialogue. They pledged to re-evaluate this temporary boycott based on conditions on the ground; the opposition had not returned to the dialogue by the end of the year.

Section 1. Respect for the Integrity of the Person, Including Freedom from:

a. Arbitrary or Unlawful Deprivation of Life

There were a number of reports that government security forces committed arbitrary or unlawful killings. In 2012 the government established the SIU to investigate and refer cases of arbitrary or unlawful killings to courts. By December the government reported the SIU referred 39 cases with 95 defendants to courts, resulting in 15 acquittals, 13 convictions, and 11 pending cases. It was unclear if the courts enforced any of the sentences and if security officers were actually in prison following sentencing. Local human rights organizations linked dozens of deaths either directly or indirectly to security forces. Local umbrella human rights group Bahrain Human Rights Observatory reported two deaths from injuries due to beating or torture and two from birdshot, and it attributed six deaths to exposure to tear gas. The government also reported two civilians died in clashes with police. Human Rights Watch reported that at least 80 individuals had died in protests since 2011. In near nightly clashes in some communities, protesters used improvised explosive devices, Molotov cocktails, and other improvised weapons, resulting in the deaths of three police officers.

On February 14, 16-year-old Hussain al-Jazeeri died after security forces fired at him with bird shot during an early morning protest. Later in February authorities detained two police officers suspected of killing al-Jazeeri pending an investigation into his death. On March 4, the court extended their detention in custody for 20 days, and for 45 more days on April 9. On May 24, the court released the two officers from custody on a 500 dinars ($1,350) bail pending trial. The next hearing date was not announced by year's end. Also injured on February 14, al-Jazeeri's relative, Mahmood al-Jazeeri, died due to head injuries from a tear gas canister fired at close range during clashes in Daih. The director general of the Central Governorate Police Station announced that investigations showed Mahmood al-Jazeeri was injured and treated at an unknown location, 24 hours prior to his arrival at the hospital. The Ministry of Health announced that examinations and X-rays showed Mahmood suffered a head injury but that a specialized physician did not treat the injury with stitches. The ministry also announced Mahmood had a fracture in the left side of his skull that caused a cerebral hemorrhage.

On November 24, the High Criminal Court of Appeals acquitted a police officer accused in the death of Salah Abbas Habib, who was found dead on a rooftop following a night of protests in April 2012. The Ministry of Interior announced Habib died under "suspicious circumstances" and launched an investigation. A local neurosurgeon not affiliated with the government conducted an independent autopsy of Habib and found injuries consistent with physical abuse, including a fractured skull, ribs, and clavicle, as well as dislocation of the cervical spine, internal bleeding, and birdshot injuries over much of the body.

Local human rights groups reported five deaths between February and October caused by complications from tear gas exposure.

On January 27 Nawaf Hamza, the head of the SIU in the Public Prosecutor's Office, announced that a female citizen reported the death of her eight-year-old child. She claimed the child died from inhaling tear gas dispersed by security forces. The child was reportedly transferred to Salmaniya Medical Complex for treatment and died on January 26. The Public Prosecutor's Office investigated and requested a medical examiner to determine the cause of death. Authorities stated the child was admitted to the hospital on January 19, following breathing problems due to severe pneumonia. The medical examiner stated in his medical report that there was no criminal cause of death.

In September 2012 a court acquitted two security personnel, Bahraini police officer Ahmed al-Thawadi and Yemeni police officer Ahmed Areen, in the 2011 deaths of protesters Ali al-Mumin and Isa Abdulhasan. On February 24, the High Criminal Court of Appeals upheld the acquittals.

The government charged Ministry of Interior (MOI) riot police officer Hasan Abdulla Hasan Khairi in 2012 with "shooting without the intent to kill" in the 2011 death of protester Ali Abdulhadi al-Mushaima. On January 31, the High Criminal Court sentenced Khairi to seven years in prison for the crime. On October 21, the High Criminal Court of Appeals reduced Khairi's sentence from seven to three years' imprisonment.

In 2012 the government charged MOI security personnel Mohammed Shar al-Hamza and Abdulhafedh Mana Ali Hamaysan with "killing without the intent to murder" in the 2011 death of protester Fadhel al-Matrook. On February 26, the High Criminal Court acquitted the two officers. On March 7, the SIU appealed the lower court's decision. On May 26, the High Criminal Court of Appeals upheld the acquittal.

In the case of Hani Abdulaziz Jumaa, who died in 2011 from gunshot injuries after being pursued by riot police, the public prosecutor initially charged Lieutenant Mohammed al-Khashram with manslaughter, which was increased to murder by the High Criminal Court. In September 2012 the High Criminal Court judges found al-Khashram guilty of "beating, leading to death," a charge similar to manslaughter, and sentenced him to seven years' imprisonment. Jumaa's family announced they would appeal the decision. On May 26, the High Criminal Court of Appeals reduced the sentence from seven years to six months.

The government claimed it held police officer defendants in a special jail reserved for security officers, but human rights activists maintained that defendants continued to serve as law enforcement officers.

b. Disappearance

There were no reports of politically motivated disappearances.

c. Torture and Other Cruel, Inhuman, or Degrading Treatment or Punishment

The constitution prohibits "harm[ing] an accused person physically or mentally." On September 3, the king issued a royal decree establishing the Commission of the Rights of Prisoners and Detainees, which the government described as an "independent national mechanism that allows monitoring prisons, detention centers and detainees" consistent with the National Preventive Mechanism established by

States Party to the Optional Protocol to the UN Convention against Torture. Nevertheless, domestic and international human rights organizations reported numerous instances of torture and other cruel, inhuman, or degrading treatment or punishment. Detainees reported to local human rights activists that security officials continued to use abusive tactics. They alleged that security officials beat them, sometimes while they were blindfolded. There was at least one report alleging they were subjected to electric shocks, simulated drowning, sexual harassment, threat of rape, and sleep deprivation. Officials reportedly placed detainees in solitary confinement, sometimes in extreme temperatures. Detainees claimed officials used excessive amounts of pepper spray and tear gas in detention centers. Human rights organizations reported authorities prevented some detainees from using toilet facilities, drinking, and eating. Other reports noted a similar pattern of abuse following arrest, including beating without interrogation, beating with interrogation, harassment, and intimidation without further physical abuse. Most detainees were Shia.

Local human rights groups, including the unlicensed Bahrain Center for Human Rights (BCHR), Bahrain Human Rights Society (BHRS), and the Shia opposition society al-Wifaq's Freedom and Human Rights Department reported that authorities beat and tortured detainees, including youth, during interrogations and denied medical treatment to injured or ill detainees. Reports indicated that the MOI interrogated detainees about illegal protest activity. Detainees reported mistreatment at official interrogation facilities. The most frequently cited locations for mistreatment included the following MOI facilities: the Adliya Criminal Investigation Division (CID), Isa Town Detention Center for Women, Dry Dock Detention Center, and Jaw Prison. Other official detention facilities less commonly cited included police stations in al-Rifaa, al-Qudaibiya, Samaheej, al-Nuaim, Nabih Saleh, al-Budaiya, and Sitra.

Local human rights groups reported that detainees also complained of abuse and torture at various unofficial temporary facilities. The most common techniques included blindfolding detainees; beating, punching, and hitting them with rubber hoses, cables, pieces of metal, wooden planks, or other objects; electric shock; exposure to extreme temperatures; stress positions; verbal abuse; threats to rape the detainee or family members; sexual assault; preventing detainees from praying; sleep deprivation; and insulting the detainee's religious sect (Shia). Victims also reported security officials used physical and psychological mistreatment to extract confessions and statements under duress or as retribution and punishment. Detainees also reported security forces abused them in their homes.

On June 12, local human rights organizations expressed concern over a YouTube video allegedly uploaded by a security forces officer. In the video the officer allegedly interrogated a shirtless man. The BCHR reported the detainee, who identified himself as Hussain Jameel Jafer Ali Marhoon, had bruises on his arm. The MOI announced it would launch an immediate investigation into the video. On September 15, the High Criminal Court released a police officer suspected in the case. It was unclear when the officer was initially detained. On September 16, SIU chief Nawaf Hamza announced the SIU filed a request to arrest the accused officer pending trial. The next hearing was scheduled for December 10 but adjourned to February 2014.

On July 12, human rights organizations expressed concern over the well-being and safety of Naji Fateel, a blogger and human rights activist, after local human rights groups released photographs showing marks on his body consistent with torture. According to human rights groups, authorities subjected Fateel to electric shocks, beating, simulated drowning, sexual harassment, the threat of rape, sleep deprivation, and standing for long periods of time while in detention at the CID and Dry Dock prison.

In February 2012 Public Prosecutor Ali al-Buainain announced the SIU would investigate allegations of torture and mistreatment of detainees by government officials. Five of the eight SIU members were former MOI prosecutors. The attorney general has the power to refer any cases deemed appropriate to the SIU. According to press reports, the SIU completed dozens of reviews and referred a similar number of cases to court. The High Criminal Court of Appeals acquitted one ruling family member and one high-ranking MOI official of torture. There was no indication that any other officials were held responsible or prosecuted for overseeing or committing acts leading to abuse, mistreatment, torture, or death. Members of the SIU visited several prisons throughout the year and referred prisoners to medical examiners when appropriate.

In June 2012 security forces officer Ali al-Shaiba was convicted and sentenced for permanently disabling a protester by shooting him in the leg with birdshot. In September 2012 the local press reported that the High Criminal Court suspended al-Shaiba's sentence "because his health condition makes it difficult to keep him in jail." In November 2012 the High Criminal Court reduced his initial sentence from five years' to three years' imprisonment. On April 14, the Supreme Court of Appeals reduced al-Shaiba's sentence from three years to six months in prison.

According to media reports, in May 2012 authorities arrested Adnan al-Mansi and charged him with criminal arson. Officials reportedly subjected al-Mansi to severe physical torture, including beatings to his head that left him temporarily paralyzed. Officials also reportedly forced him to stand in the sun for hours, denying him access to toilet facilities, water, and adequate medical treatment. Authorities brought al-Mansi's case before the High Criminal Court in December 2012; hearings were held on March 3 and October 29. On December 2, the High Criminal Court convicted and sentenced him to seven years' imprisonment. His appeal was scheduled for February 2014.

The government did not fully pursue investigations into cases of torture and mistreatment during the 2011 State of National Safety (SNS), as documented by the BICI, and not all individuals committing these acts were held accountable. During the year the government prosecuted some members of the security forces on charges related to deaths in detention and abuses that took place during the SNS.

In December 2012 the High Criminal Court sentenced two Bahrain National Security Agency (BNSA) police officers each to seven years in prison for torturing to death Abdul Karim Fakhrawi, cofounder of *Al-Wasat* newspaper. In 2011 police detained, beat, and tortured Fakhrawi in jail; he died as a result. On June 16, the High Criminal Court of Appeal adjourned the trial to September 8 and then to October 27. On October 27, the court reduced the sentences of the two officers from seven years to three years' imprisonment each.

The trial of five Pakistani police officers employed by the MOI--Abdulrashid Rasool Bakhsh, Mohammed Ihsan Muthaffar, Riyadh Shahid Habib Allah, Rahat Adeel Mohammed, and Khalid Iqbal Mohammed Iqbal--for the 2011 deaths of detainees Zakariya al-Asheeri and Ali Saqer continued during the year. On March 2, the High Criminal Court sentenced Bakhsh and Muthaffar to 10 years' imprisonment each for beating Saqer to death "without the intent to kill." The other three accused were acquitted in Saqer's case. On September 29, the High Criminal Court of Appeals reduced the sentences from 10 to five years in prison for both officers. The court acquitted all five accused police officers of charges of inflicting a beating that led to al-Asheeri's death.

Authorities continued investigating the case of medical personnel who filed a motion alleging torture while in CID custody in 2011. Torture included electric shocks, beatings, and threats of rape or injury to family members. Prosecutors initially investigated 15 security personnel over the allegations. In October 2012 the Public Prosecutor's Office charged two officers, Mubarak bin Huwail and Shaikha Noora bint Ebrahim al-Khalifa, with torture. On July 1, the High Criminal Court acquitted the two officers. On December 23, the High Criminal Court of Appeals upheld the verdict.

Children were also subjected to torture and other cruel, inhuman, or degrading treatment or punishment. Human rights groups reported that authorities detained children, sometimes under the age of 15 (the maximum age the penal code considers a person a child), and subjected them to various forms of mistreatment, including beating, slapping, kicking, lashing with rubber hoses, threats of sexual assault, burning with cigarettes, and verbal abuse. Local human rights group Bahrain Human Rights Observatory reported in September that authorities had detained 101 children since January. Human rights activists reported that at least one child was under the age of 13.

On August 11, authorities arrested 13-year-old Salman Mahdi Salman and detained him for 27 days. Amnesty International (AI) reported that the government charged him with carrying a Molotov cocktail and a cigarette lighter and wearing a mask at the time of his arrest. AI also reported that authorities beat and tortured him at Budaiya Police Station to force him to confess to his charges. On September 11, authorities released him. A court scheduled hearings for September 26 and November 28. His next hearing was scheduled for January 30, 2014.

According to an AI report, police arrested two juveniles, Jehad Sadeq Aziz Salman, and Ebrahim Ahmed Radi al-Meqdad, during a July 2012 protest in the Bilad al-Qadeem neighborhood of Manama. The report noted the two juveniles were not allowed to contact their families for nearly 48 hours after their arrests and were interrogated without a lawyer present. According to AI the youths told their families that police beat them in detention. Authorities charged the youths with intent to murder, burning a police car, illegally gathering and rioting, throwing Molotov cocktails, and attempting to steal a police car. On April 4, according to AI, the High Criminal Court sentenced Salman and al-Meqdad each to 10 years' imprisonment for charges associated with the antiterrorism law. Their lawyers appealed, and on September 29, the High Criminal Court of Appeals upheld the guilty verdict. On October 29, their defense lawyer filed a request for appeal with the Court of Cassation but no update was available on the appeal request at year's end.

Prison and Detention Center Conditions

There were conflicting reports on conditions in prisons and detention centers, with human rights activists claiming harsh and sometimes life-threatening conditions, while government officials disputed these charges. There were multiple reports from detainees and human rights organizations of substandard conditions and abuse in official detention centers as well as reports of substandard conditions at the long-term Jaw Prison. Human rights groups alleged authorities mistreated youth at Jaw Prison. The SIU met with prominent detainees and claimed medical experts examined them. There were scores of reports of abuse at unofficial short-term detention centers. On November 25, the Ombudsman's Office reported that authorities placed juveniles between the ages of 15 and 18 in cells separate from other detainees.

Physical Conditions: According to the government, in 2012 prison facilities held 1,297 convicted male prisoners, 75 female prisoners, and 53 juvenile prisoners. There were also 845 pretrial male detainees and 37 female detainees. The government claimed convicted prisoners and pretrial detainees were held in separate facilities. Human rights observers reported juveniles and adults were sometimes held in the same facilities.

In September the Office of the Ombudsman reported that Jaw Prison had the capacity for 1,200 prisoners but held 1,608. Of the prisoners classed as juveniles (between 15 to 21 years old), it had facilities for 72 but held 154 inmates The report recommended urgent action be taken to address the overcrowding and that juveniles between 15 and 18 in separate facilities from the 19- to 21-year-old inmates. The report asserted that prison documents distributed to prisoners did not fully cover all of the prisoners' legal rights.

No statistics were available on the prevalence of death in prisons, although there were reports that prisoners died as a result of inadequate medical care. There were no reports of deaths in prison of pretrial detainees during the year.

On September 23, detainee Ali al-Nashmi was reportedly transferred to a hospital in a coma. Al-Nashmi died on September 27, and his lawyer reported prison officials did not properly care for the detainee or provide him proper medical treatment. The Public Prosecutor's Office reported al-Nashmi died of HIV/AIDS-linked complications.

Although the government reported during the year that potable water was available for all detainees and there were water coolers in all detention centers, there were reports of lack of access to water for drinking and washing, lack of shower facilities and soap, and unhygienic toilet facilities. Detainees were sometimes subjected to extreme temperatures or held in solitary confinement. Other detainees complained they were denied necessary medical treatment, prevented from visiting with family, and denied communication with legal representation. In many cases detainees and lawyers said they were not allowed sufficient, consistent access to their legal counsel and clients, which resulted in inadequate consultations to prepare their defense. Other detainees reported physical abuse, verbal assault, and threats of sexual assault. In 2012 the Bahrain Rehabilitation and Anti-Violence Organization documented witness testimonies regarding conditions at detention facilities, including complaints by several detainees that they were refused access to toilet facilities for long periods, most often at the CID and al-Asri short-term detention centers.

In May the wife of activist and BCHR president Nabeel Rajab publicly complained of poor conditions for her husband at Jaw Prison, including denial of independent medical care, limited communication with family and legal counsel, and isolated quarters. In June an SIU member met with Rajab and ordered that he visit a government medical consultant. According to the BCHR, Rajab telephoned his wife on May 14 to report the torture of eight young prisoners and requested a meeting with the International Committee of the Red Cross (ICRC) to report his testimony. In December the SIU questioned 13 detainees and referred 11 police officers to court for abusing detainees. In September the Ombudsman's Office visited Jaw Prison and met with Rajab.

In May lawyers for Ali al-Ekri and Ibrahim al-Dimistani, physicians imprisoned during the 2011 unrest, reported the two did not receive adequate medical care in Jaw Prison. They also claimed mistreatment at the Bahrain Defense Force Hospital.

Administration: It was unclear whether recordkeeping on prisoners was adequate. Officials from the Ombudsman's Office were available to respond to complaints. Community service was proposed as an alternative to sentencing for nonviolent offenders, but it was unknown if such sentencing had been implemented. Prisoners had access to visitors at least once a month, often more frequently, except in instances when prisoners were denied access to visitors for refusing to wear prison uniforms. Prisoners were permitted religious services and could file complaints to judicial authorities without censorship, although there were reports that prisoners were sometimes not able to communicate with lawyers and family members.

Independent Monitoring: Representatives from the ICRC and Red Crescent were granted access to prison facilities throughout the year. According to media reports, the ICRC visited detention centers and Jaw Prison. According to the government, several international organizations and nongovernmental organization (NGO) personnel also received access to detention centers to monitor detainee conditions during the year. These included Human Rights Watch and a delegation from the EU parliament. The government indefinitely postponed the visit of the UN special rapporteur on torture, Juan Mendez, during the year.

Improvements: The SIU, formed in February 2012, acted as a mechanism for the public to lodge complaints about prisoner mistreatment or conditions in prisons and detention facilities. The SIU investigated approximately 15 cases and referred several others to court. The Office of the Ombudsman began monitoring prisons and detention centers when it opened to the public in July, and it accepted written and in-person complaints. As of November the office had received approximately 36 complaints, and the SIU reported that individuals filed 16 additional complaints of torture and mistreatment in December.

Various ministries within the government reported improved facilities and conditions inside detention centers and prisons. In December government officials reported they had installed recording equipment in 26 interrogation rooms and signed an agreement with a German company to equip 60 additional interrogation rooms. It was unclear whether cameras had been installed in all police stations by year's end. Police installed cameras on MOI vehicles and at official checkpoints.

In an effort to ensure prisoners were aware of their rights and being held in safe and legal conditions, the Ombudsman's Office monitored detention centers and corrections facilities and conducted announced and unannounced visits to prisons.

d. Arbitrary Arrest or Detention

The constitution prohibits arbitrary arrest and detention. There were reports from local and international human rights groups, however, of arbitrary arrests and detention. Local human rights organizations reported hundreds of arbitrary arrests and estimated that more than 1,000 arrested detainees awaited trial. Human rights groups claimed the MOI conducted the majority of house arrests without presenting an arrest warrant. Government sources disputed these claims. In August 2012 Senior Public Prosecutor Wael Bualley announced that 923 individuals were in detention and 595 faced prosecution related to the 2011 unrest.

On July 28, members from the Council of Representatives and Shura Council, along with 12 ministers, met in an extraordinary parliamentary session. The two bodies jointly sent 22 recommendations to the king, which he accepted and decreed on July 31. These recommendations tightened penalties for those involved in terrorism, banned demonstrations in the capital, allowed for legal action against political associations accused of inciting and supporting violence and terrorism, and granted security services powers to protect society from terrorism, including the ability to declare a State of National Safety. The MOI arrested, detained, and charged individuals in accordance with these new laws.

Role of the Police and Security Apparatus

The MOI is responsible for internal security and controls the public security force and specialized security units responsible for maintaining internal order. The coast guard is under the jurisdiction of the MOI. The Bahrain Defense Force (BDF) is primarily responsible for defending against external threats, while the Bahrain National Guard is responsible for defending against external threats and is a security force against internal threats.

In February 2012 the king issued decrees to establish an independent ombudsman's office at the MOI and create an independent office for the inspector general at the BNSA. In August 2012 the MOI announced the appointment of Nawaf al-Ma'awada as ombudsman. These independent offices were responsible for addressing cases of mistreatment and abuse; they were operational throughout the year. It was unclear what role the BNSA's inspector general played in investigating complaints. The MOI Ombudsman's Office began official operations in July.

Security forces were not completely effective in maintaining order and were often accused of using excessive force, but they showed greater restraint in comparison with its conduct in response to protests in 2011. Many human rights groups continued to assert that investigations into police abuse were slow and ineffective.

The Bahrain News Agency reported in March 2012 that the interior minister approved the BICI's recommendation for a new code of conduct for police that requires officers to abide by 10 principles, including limited use of force and zero tolerance for torture and mistreatment. According to government officials, the code is consistent with international human rights standards and forbids the use of force "except when absolutely necessary." The Royal Police Academy included the code in its curriculum in 2012 and provided new recruits with copies in English and Arabic. It was unclear whether the MOI enforced the code of conduct throughout the year.

The MOI Ombudsman's Office maintained a hotline for citizens to report police abuse, but many Shia hesitated to report abuse for fear of retribution. The government reported in 2012 that the hotline received 872 complaints, not all of which were directly related to police abuse. During the year the government revised the process through which they would accept complaints and began to use the hotline as a means of informing people how to submit an official complaint through a paper format.

Starting in 2012 the Ministry of Interior participated in training courses at the International Institute of Higher Studies in Criminal Sciences in Siracusa, Italy. The government reported 34 judges, prosecutors, and investigators took part in three training courses held during the year.

According to the government's November 2012 BICI follow-up report, 100 female and 255 male recruits were hired in the first round of community policing recruitment to perform police work in all ministry departments. On June 9, the government stated that 577 police graduated and the majority would be "working in the community." One of the new officers reported that approximately 75 percent of the class were Shia officers.

Arrest Procedures and Treatment of Detainees

The law stipulates that law enforcement officials may arrest without a warrant individuals who are caught committing a felony or misdemeanor punishable by a prison term of more than three months, should sufficient evidence be available to press charges. The law further stipulates that in other cases, should sufficient evidence exist to charge a person with a felony, theft, fraud, serious assault, or possession or acquisition of illegal narcotics, law enforcement officers may arrest the person without a warrant. Local activists reported that this process was not always enforced.

By law an arrested individual must be interrogated immediately by the arresting authority and cannot be detained for more than 48 hours, after which the detainee must either be released or transferred to the Public Prosecution for further questioning. The Public Prosecution is required to question the detainee within 24 hours, and the detainee has the right to legal counsel during questioning. To hold the detainee longer, the Public Prosecution must issue a formal detention order based on the charges against the detainee. Detention may be extended for a period of up to seven days for further questioning. If any further extension is required, the detainee must be brought before a judge, who may authorize a further extension not exceeding 45 days. Any extensions beyond that must be authorized by the High Criminal Court and renewed at 45-day intervals. In the case of alleged acts of terror, law enforcement officials may detain individuals for five days, with a 10-day extension granted by the Public Prosecution, and the initial detention authorized by the Public Prosecution can be 60 days. There was a functioning system of bail that provided maximum and minimum bail amounts based on the charges. The bail law allows the presiding judge to determine the amount within these parameters on a case-by-case basis. In most cases attorneys must seek a court order to confer with clients. The state provided counsel to indigent detainees.

According to reports by local and international human rights groups, some detainees were held for weeks with limited access to the outside world. There were cases in which detainees were denied access to lawyers, sometimes for long periods and at times until the day of their trials. The government sometimes withheld information from detainees and their families about the detainees' whereabouts for days or weeks. In a few cases, the government failed to acknowledge it was holding individuals in detention for a period of days. In contrast with 2012, some detainees were held incommunicado for weeks or months.

Arbitrary Arrest: The MOI (in particular the CID and the Public Security Forces, which include the riot police) arbitrarily arrested numerous individuals. Human rights activists cited 291 arrests in May and 188 arrests in July. Activists estimated that between February and September, the MOI arrested 1,392 citizens, including 92 children and 13 women. Many detained individuals reported being arrested but not shown warrants by arresting forces. There were many reports that security forces raided homes and damaged property without providing compensation while searching for suspected criminals.

On September 17, MOI officers arrested the al-Wifaq society's chief political advisor, Khalil Marzooq, and interrogated him in the presence of his lawyer at Budaiya Police Station and the General Public Prosecutor's Office. The Public Prosecution ordered Marzooq's detention for 30 days pending investigation into charges of inciting terrorism and violence after delivering a speech where he called on individuals to refrain from violence. On October 24, authorities released Marzooq on condition that he not leave the country and adjourned his trial until

November 18. A hearing scheduled for December 12 was postponed until January 2014 to hear the witnesses for the defense.

In July 2012 security forces arrested Fakhriya Ahmed and her Pakistani husband and raided their home; the couple was accused of hiding activists sought by authorities. Ahmed and her husband were arraigned in September 2012 on charges of "hiding a wanted felon," and the court released them two weeks later on bail of 100 dinars ($270). The case remained open with no legal action taken during the year.

e. Denial of Fair Public Trial

Although the constitution provides for an independent judiciary, the king controls the judicial system. In accordance with the constitution, the king appoints all judges by royal decree. He formerly served as the chairperson of the Supreme Judicial Council, the body responsible for supervising the work of the courts, and as the public prosecutor. In September, however, he issued a royal decree appointing Salem al-Kawari as the chairperson. Al-Kawari previously served as the head of the Constitutional Court. In 2011 the government used a hybrid military-civilian court to try civilians, including opposition leaders, political activists, rights activists, and others who supported or were perceived as supporting the protest movement. Following recommendations put forward in the BICI, cases heard in the military-civilian court were retried in civilian courts, but some of the trials had not been completed by year's end, and there were widespread accusations the judiciary was highly politicized and not independent.

In the high-profile trial of 13 political activists charged with attempting to overthrow the regime, defense attorneys and local and international human rights groups noted a number of irregularities. In July 2012 the head judge placed a gag order on media coverage and declared all further sessions closed. Defense lawyers noted that confessions extracted through torture remained admissible in court. They also asserted the verdicts were politically motivated and based on the defendants' opposition to the government. On January 7, the Court of Cassation upheld the convictions of the 13 political activists. The court sentenced seven of the 13 activists to life sentences, four to 15 years in prison, and two to five years' imprisonment. Members of the defendants' families reported they were not permitted to attend the trial.

On December 2, the High Criminal Court of Appeals refused to grant BCHR president Nabeel Rajab an early release as permitted by law after serving 75 percent of his sentence. In August 2012 authorities convicted Rajab on three separate counts of "illegal gathering" (participating in an illegal protest or demonstration), receiving three one-year imprisonment sentences. By comparison lawyers reported that many protesters charged with illegal gathering received sentences ranging from 45 days to three months in prison. In December 2012 the High Criminal Court reduced Rajab's sentence from three years to two years: one year for the first charge, six months for the second, and six months for the third charge of illegal gathering.

Trial Procedures

According to the constitution, defendants are presumed innocent until proven guilty. There is a right to be informed promptly and in detail of charges. By law detainees should be informed about the charges against them upon arrest. Civil and criminal trial procedures provide for a public trial. There are no jury trials. Rulings are made by a panel of three judges. Defendants have the right to prompt consultation with an attorney of their choice within 48 hours (unless they are charged pursuant to counterterrorism legislation). The government provided counsel at public expense to indigent defendants. No law governs defendants' access to government-held evidence, and such evidence was available at the discretion of the court. Defendants have the right to present witnesses and evidence on their behalf and question witnesses against them. Defendants are not compelled to testify or to confess guilt and have the right to appeal.

Women's legal rights varied according to Shia or Sunni interpretations of Islamic law (see section 6).

Political Prisoners and Detainees

Human rights organizations reported that many of those arrested were targeted because of their political activism.

According to local human rights groups, many individuals were detained or imprisoned for activities related to the unrest. A number of the political detainees from 2011 were leaders or prominent members of political groups and societies. These included Ibrahim Sharif, secretary general of the secular Wa'ad political society, and Shaikh Mohammed Ali al-Mahfoodh, secretary general of the dissolved Shia opposition political society Amal. Many of these political detainees remained in prison throughout the year. In September 2012 the Higher Appellate Court upheld Sharif's five-year sentence on charges that included participating in a plot to overthrow the regime. On January 7, the Court of Cassation upheld the verdict. In November 2012 al-Mahfoodh's appeal of his 10-year sentence on charges that included "seeking to overthrow the regime by force, inciting public hatred, and spreading false news" continued in the High Criminal Court of Appeals, and his sentence was reduced from 10 years to five years. Both men remained imprisoned at year's end.

Some political prisoners did not receive access to international human rights organizations, although authorities allowed others to meet with representatives of select human rights and humanitarian organizations.

Civil Judicial Procedures and Remedies

Citizens may bring civil suits before a court seeking cessation of or damages for some types of human rights violations. In many such situations, however, the law prevents citizens from filing civil suits against security agencies.

According to the December BICI follow-up report, authorities compensated 39 death cases, with families receiving 2.34 million dinars ($6.3 million). Thirty-five cases were cited in the BICI report, and four additional cases, according to the compensation committee, merited compensation. Local human rights activists reported that the government provided compensation only for deaths that occurred in 2011. In addition to deaths, there were 421 applications for compensation for injuries; 193 cases were selected for the first phase, and the Civil Settlement Office assessed the settlement value of each claim based on the percentage of permanent disability determined by a medical examiner. There were reports from human rights activists that some families refused to accept the compensation due to conditions placed upon the funds.

f. Arbitrary Interference with Privacy, Family, Home, or Correspondence

Although the constitution prohibits such actions, the government violated these prohibitions. Human rights organizations reported that security forces entered homes without authorization and destroyed or confiscated personal property, including cars, electronics, and furniture. Reports indicated that security forces failed to identify themselves, inform the arrested individual of the reasons for arrest, show arrest warrants, or inform family members of the reasons for arrest or location of arrested individuals, and they acted in an aggressive and at times terrorizing manner towards individuals in households. At least one activist reported 450 houses were raided in July and August and 120 houses raided in November.

The government is required to obtain a court order before monitoring telephone calls, e-mail, and personal correspondence. Many local opposition groups believed the government monitored the activities of individuals and groups deemed to threaten national security. Many Shia citizens and human rights organizations believed there were extensive police informer networks.

Reports also indicated the government used computer programming to spy on political activists and members of the opposition inside and outside the country.

According to local and international human rights groups, security officials threatened detainees' family members with reprisals, including sexual assault, for the detainee's unwillingness to cooperate during interrogations and refusal to sign confession statements.

Security forces also threatened individuals if they were believed to constitute a risk to national security.

Section 2. Respect for Civil Liberties, Including:

a. Freedom of Speech and Press

The constitution provides for freedom of speech and press, "provided that the fundamental beliefs of Islamic doctrine are not infringed, the unity of the people is not prejudiced, and discord and sectarianism are not aroused." The government limited freedom of speech and press through active prosecution of individuals under libel, slander, and national security laws; targeting civilian and professional journalists; and proposing legislation to limit speech in print and social media.

Freedom of Speech: The law forbids any speech that infringes on public order or morals. While individuals openly expressed critical opinions regarding domestic political and social issues in private settings, those who publicly expressed such opinions often faced repercussions. The government reported that it dropped and no longer pursued charges or cases involving freedom of expression following BICI recommendations. During the year, however, the government suppressed acts of civil disobedience, which included critical speech, under charges of unlawful assembly. Lawyers asserted that, as in the trial of 13 political activists convicted of attempting to overthrow the regime in 2011, prosecutors continued to pursue charges against their clients related to public expression.

In March the government arrested five individuals for "insulting the king" on Twitter. They were tried and convicted; their sentences ranged from six months to one year's imprisonment. Dozens were arrested for "inciting protests" on Twitter. Individuals arrested for "insulting the king" and for "inciting protests" continued to appeal their convictions and sentences at the end of the year.

On September 12, the High Criminal Court of Appeals upheld the acquittal of the BCHR head of monitoring, Sayed Yousif al-Muhafadha, earlier charged with "spreading false information on Twitter." On March 11, the Lower Criminal Court had acquitted al-Muhafadha of the charge, but the Public Prosecution appealed the decision. Authorities first arrested al-Muhafadha in December 2012 and held him in custody for seven days. Later in December 2012, he was brought before the Public Prosecution and subsequently referred to the Lower Criminal Court where his detention continued until January 17, when the court granted his provisional release and fined him 100 dinars ($270).

Press Freedoms: The government did not own any print media, but the Information Affairs Authority (IAA) and other government entities exercised considerable control over privately owned domestic print media.

The government owned and operated all domestic radio and television stations. Audiences generally received radio and television broadcasts in Arabic, Farsi, and English from countries in the region, including by satellite without interference. The IAA reviewed all books and publications prior to issuing printing licenses. The Ministry of Justice and Islamic Affairs reviewed books that discussed religion.

Violence and Harassment: According to local journalists, between January and October there were 62 reports of journalists being harassed, arrested, or attacked due to their reporting. The government refused visas to some international media representatives.

AI reported that on July 31, plainclothes police arrested blogger Mohammed Hassan Sadef and cameraman Hussain Habib without a warrant and did not permit them access to a lawyer or their families. The MOI released Sadef on October 3; Habib remained detained at year's end awaiting trial.

In February, Dubai Airport authorities banned the editor in chief of *Al-Wasat* newspaper, Mansoor al-Jamri, and his wife, Associated Press reporter Reem Khalifa, from entering the United Arab Emirates. The authorities did not reveal the cause of the ban, but unofficial sources said that authorities distributed lists at the beginning of the year with the names of several Bahrainis banned from travel to limit their activities within the Gulf Cooperation Council States.

In April 2012 Colin Freeman with the *Sunday Telegraph* reported that he and his Bahraini colleague Mohammed Hasan were "stopped and arrested on suspicion of attending an illegal demonstration" but later released. On July 21, authorities arrested Hasan and detained him at the CID until August 4; he remained detained at Dry Docks based on accusations that he was a member of the violent opposition group February 14 Youth Coalition. Hasan alleged security officials tortured him; authorities released him on October 3.

Bahraini photojournalist Mazen Mahdi of European Pressphoto Agency reported that riot police threatened to break his camera and arrest him on multiple occasions for filming protests. In December 2012 authorities arrested Mahdi but released him an hour later. On February 14, authorities detained Mahdi and two other journalists without charge and released them the same day.

In September 2012 the High Criminal Court heard witness testimony on the alleged abuse of journalist Nazeeha Saeed during her detention and interrogation in May 2011. In October 2012 the court acquitted Sarah Mohammed, the female police officer charged with the abuse. Saeed appealed and on June 24, the High Criminal Court of Appeal upheld the acquittal. Saeed requested that the Public Prosecutor's Office file another appeal on her behalf, but the office did not take further action.

Censorship or Content Restrictions: Government censorship occurred. IAA personnel actively monitored and blocked stories on matters deemed sensitive, especially those related to sectarianism, national security, or criticism of the royal family, the Saudi royal family, or the judiciary. Journalists widely practiced self-censorship. In 2012 some members of the media reported government officials contacted editors directly and told them to stop writing about certain subjects or told them not to publish a press release or a story.

Government authorities continued to ban several books that were part of the country's international book fair, held in March and April 2012. Index on Censorship, an international NGO that supports freedom of expression, reported the IAA's Press and Publications Directorate banned and confiscated all copies of the book *Political Organizations and Societies in Bahrain*, coauthored by Bahraini writer Abbas Almurshid, and another book by Almurshid, *Bahrain in the Gulf Gazetteer*. Additionally, a number of books remained banned from 2010, including the Arabic translation of *The Personal Diary of Charles Belgrave* and *Unbridled Hatreds: Reading in the Fate of Ancient Hatreds*, by Bahraini author Nader Kadim.

On September 12, the Ministry of Information Affairs announced that it banned books "linked to Hezbollah" because the banned books carried "sectarian and ideological poisons," were written about Hezbollah, or published by publishing houses linked to Hezbollah.

Libel Laws/National Security: The government enforced libel and national security-related laws restricting freedom of the press. The penal code prohibits libel, slander, and "divulging secrets" and stipulates a punishment of imprisonment for no more than two years or a fine of no more than 200 dinars ($540). Application of the slander law was selective. National security-related law provides for fines of as much as 10,000 dinars ($27,000) and prison sentences of at least six months for criticizing the king or inciting actions that undermine state security, as well as fines of up to 2,000 dinars ($5,400) for 14 related offenses. Punishable activities include publicizing statements issued by a foreign state or organization before obtaining the consent of the IAA, publishing any reports that may adversely affect the dinar's value, reporting any offense against a head of a state that maintains diplomatic relations with the country, and publishing offensive remarks about an accredited representative of a foreign country because of acts connected with the person's position.

In June 2012 authorities arrested BCHR president Nabeel Rajab and charged him with libel after a group of retired BDF army and MOI security officers filed a complaint over another Twitter posting in which they claimed Rajab "insulted the people of Muharraq." Later that month he was released on bail after defense attorneys submitted a letter signed by 400 Muharraq residents claiming they did not find Rajab's statements insulting. In July 2012 the Lower Criminal Court found Rajab guilty of the charge and sentenced him to three months in prison. Rajab appealed and was acquitted in August 2012, but he remained in prison after being convicted of illegal gathering.

Internet Freedom

The government restricted internet freedom and monitored individuals' online activities, including via social media, leading to legal action and punishment of some individuals during the year.

In September 2012 the MOI announced efforts to clamp down on online smear campaigns and slandering. The ministry urged citizens to report cyber violations to a ministry website to permit legal actions against slanderers and their web platforms and stop cyber defamation. The acting general director of Corruption Combating and Electronic and Economic Security claimed an alarming increase in cyber defamation; the misuse of communication technologies prompted the ministry's action. Members of civil society expressed concern regarding the new measures and reported that the number of individuals arrested for online postings has increased.

In 2012 the governmental Telecommunications Regulatory Authority ordered service providers to block internet users' access to websites officials considered antigovernment, anti-Islamic, or likely to incite sectarian tensions. Many blocked websites featured live-streaming audio or video content. The government continued to block the websites of the BCHR, the online newspaper *Bahrain Mirror*, and the social forum *Bahrain Online*. Other websites reportedly blocked included sites that provided proxy or anonymity tools. In September 2012 the MOI announced it coordinated efforts to block any websites showing the film *Innocence of Muslims*. The MOI also encouraged all citizens to "prevent the spread of the film" by refraining from posting, uploading, or sharing the film on social media sites. On August 4, the Ministry of Communication blocked 70 websites in accordance with laws passed following Parliament's July 28 recommendations.

Academic Freedom and Cultural Events

The government restricted academic freedom and cultural events. The government dismissed professors and suspended or expelled hundreds of university students for their participation in demonstrations and political activities in 2011. The government re-instated most but not all professors dismissed as a consequence of 2011 events; however, 12 teachers remained in prison throughout the year for a variety of crimes, including the president of the Bahrain Teachers' Society, Mahdi Abu Deeb. All students not charged with violent crimes were re-instated but were required to sign loyalty pledges and received warnings not to engage in political activity on campus. Some academics engaged in self-censorship, avoiding discussion of contentious political issues.

The University of Bahrain suspended and subsequently dismissed 19 academics on charges ranging from participation in demonstrations to spreading false news in 2012; however, the government re-instated all 19 academics by the end of 2012. Human rights activists reported that re-instated teachers had been subjected to torture while detained; the government demoted them after re-instatement.

There were reports of cultural institutions declining to offer programs considered politically sensitive during the year. Human rights advocates claimed that the government unfairly distributed university scholarships. The government announced that it distributed all scholarships based on merit. On June 29, Isa al-Koohejji, Ministry of Education director of scholarships, announced the ministry had not denied a scholarship to any student with a cumulative average of 90 percent or higher.

b. Freedom of Peaceful Assembly and Association

Freedom of Assembly

The constitution provides for the right of free assembly, but the law restricts the exercise of this right. During the year security forces intervened during unauthorized demonstrations or when authorized demonstrations turned violent. According to the MOI, organizers must submit requests for permission to hold public gatherings or demonstrations at least 72 hours in advance. The law outlines the locations and times during which functions are prohibited, including areas close to hospitals, airports, commercial locations, and security-related facilities, and, further to Parliament's July 28 recommendations, inside the city of Manama. The law states that every public gathering shall have a committee comprised of a head and at least two members. The committee is responsible for supervising and preventing any illegal acts during the function. According to the law, the MOI is not obligated to provide justification as to why it approves or denies requests for protests. The penal code penalizes any gathering "of five or more individuals" that is held for the "purpose of committing crimes or inciting others to commit crimes." Lawyers asserted demonstrations should not be prevented in advance based on assumptions that crimes would be committed.

The government limited and controlled political gatherings, and it regularly denied permits for organized demonstrations. From mid-June through late August, the government stopped granting permits for protests. Additionally, on August 6, as part of Parliament's 22 recommendations during extraordinary session, it amended

Article 11 to prohibit demonstrations, marches, rallies, or sit-ins in Manama, as well as any marches or gatherings at or near hospitals, airports, shopping malls, or other places of security. The use of vehicles in any demonstration, protest, or gathering is prohibited unless a special written permission is obtained from the head of Public Security.

The government denied some gatherings and demonstrations on the basis that they would hinder traffic flow, disrupt economic activity, or were a threat to civilians. The government established a committee to identify suitable and sustainable demonstration locations, but the committee's findings were unclear. The violent opposition group February 14 Youth Coalition and other groups conducted numerous unregistered protests against the government and blocked roads with debris and tire fires, threw Molotov cocktails, employed improvised explosive devises, and shot iron bars and other projectiles at security personnel, resulting in severe injuries and civilian and police deaths.

There were a series of violent attacks against security officers and government officials during the year, killing several security officers. On February 14, police officer Mohamed Asif Khan died in Sehla after violent protesters shot him with a projectile. On April 14, there were four separate simultaneous explosions, one of which was caused by a gas cylinder placed inside a stolen car and remotely detonated. On July 6, MOI authorities reported that an improvised explosive device killed Yasser Deeb, a Pakistani Special Security Forces Command officer in Sitra, and injured two other police officers. The violent opposition group al-Ashtar Brigade claimed responsibility for the attacks. On July 15, violent protesters attacked Member of Parliament Abbas al-Mahdi's house with Molotov cocktails. On September 17, police officer Amer Abdul Khalid died from injuries suffered in an explosion in al-Dair on August 17. The trials against suspects were underway at year's end. Security forces often responded following a violent incident, sometimes with excessive force.

The law states that funeral processions may not be turned into political rallies and that security officials may be present at any public gathering. Organizers of an unauthorized gathering face prison sentences of three to six months. The minimum sentence for participating in an illegal gathering is one month, and the maximum is two years. Longer sentences are reserved for cases where violence is used in an illegal gathering. The maximum fine is 200 dinars ($540). The law regulates election campaigning and prohibits political activities at worship centers, universities, schools, government buildings, and public institutions. The government did not allow mosques, maatams (Shia religious community centers), or other religious sites to be used for political gatherings. In a case from 2011, SNS courts prosecuted Mahdi Abu Deeb and Jalila al-Salman, respectively the president and vice president of the Bahrain Teachers' Society, for conducting political activities at schools. In 2011 the SNS court convicted and sentenced Abu Deeb to a 15-year prison sentence, while al-Salman received a three-year sentence. The two appealed their sentences and claimed their confessions were obtained by torture. In October 2012 the High Criminal Court reduced Abu Deeb's sentence to five years and al-Salman's sentence to six months. Al-Salman completed her sentence, and authorities released her in November 2012. Both Abu Deeb and al-Salman filed appeals with the Court of Cassation during the year, and on July 1, the Court of Cassation rejected Abu Deeb's defense's appeal for his release and rejected al-Salman's appeal to overturn her conviction. The case continued throughout the year, and on November 25, the Court of Cassation upheld the guilty verdicts for both of the accused.

Human rights activists reported that, on April 19, during the time of the Formula One Grand Prix, clashes between protestors and police occurred in different areas of the country and left several people injured by use of tear gas. Protesters burned tires and blocked a number of roads. Al-Wifaq's Freedom and Human Rights Department cited the arrest of 26 individuals; authorities later released some of those arrested. Al-Wifaq also reported that there were several reports of suffocation due to the excessive use of tear gas in some areas. Local human rights activists reported an undetermined number of shotgun and tear gas canister injuries in Abu Saiba. There were no reports of investigations into these incidents.

Freedom of Association

The constitution provides for freedom of association, but the government limited this right. Although the government does not allow the formation of political parties, it authorized registered political societies to run candidates for office and to participate in other political activities.

On September 3, the minister of justice issued an order stipulating that political societies should coordinate their contact with foreign diplomatic or consular missions, foreign governmental organizations, or representatives of foreign governments with the Ministry of Foreign Affairs, which can elect to send a representative to the meeting. At year's end authorities had not actively enforced the order.

The government required all groups to register: civil society groups with the Ministry of Social Development, political societies with the Ministry of Justice and Islamic Affairs, and labor unions with the Ministry of Labor. The government decided whether a group was social or political in nature, based on its proposed bylaws. The law prohibits any activity by an unlicensed society as well as any political activity by a licensed civil society group. A number of unlicensed societies were active in the country.

On September 10, the prime minister issued a decree directing government agencies to take action against "unlicensed organizations that provoke terrorist acts and sow sectarianism." Following the decree the Ministry of Justice filed a lawsuit against individual members of the unlicensed Islamic Ulema Council. The trial continued at year's end with a verdict scheduled for January 2014.

To apply for registration, a political society must submit its bylaws signed by all founding members, a list of all members and copies of their residency cards, and a financial statement identifying the society's sources of funding and bank information. The society's principles, goals, and programs must not run counter to sharia or national interest, as interpreted by the judiciary, nor may the society be based on sectarian, geographic, or class identity. A number of societies operated outside of these rules, and some functioned on a sectarian basis.

A civil society group applying for registration must submit its bylaws signed by all founding members, together with minutes of the founding committee's meetings containing the names, professions, places of residence, and signatures of all founding members. The law grants the Ministry of Social Development the right to reject the registration of any civil society group if it finds the society's services unnecessary, already provided by another society, contrary to state security, or aimed at reviving a previously dissolved society. Associations whose applications are rejected or ignored may appeal to the High Civil Court, which may annul the ministry's decision or refuse the appeal.

Many NGOs and civil society activists asserted the Ministry of Social Development routinely exploited its oversight role to stymie the activities of NGOs and other civil society organizations. While some local NGOs asserted bureaucratic incompetence characterized the ministry's dealings with NGOs, many others stated that officials actively sought to undermine some groups' activities and imposed burdensome bureaucratic procedures on NGO board members and volunteers. Funding from international sources must be vetted by the Justice Ministry and Interior Ministry.

In June 2012 the Ministry of Justice filed a case against the Islamic Action (Amal) political society, commonly referred to as the Shirazi grouping, on charges that Amal "failed to convene a general conference for more than four years" and that the most recent conference was invalid because it was "held in a place of worship." The ministry also charged the society with basing its political decisions on the guidance of senior religious leaders abroad who "call for violence and incite hatred" and for not submitting a copy of its annual budget to the ministry. In July 2012 the administrative court dissolved the society and, immediately thereafter, the media reported that the government would liquidate all assets of the society. In November 2012 the High Criminal Court of Appeals adjourned the case regarding dissolution of Amal until the following year. On April 15, the High Criminal Court of Appeals upheld the verdict dissolving the society.

c. Freedom of Religion

See the Department of State's *International Religious Freedom Report* at www.state.gov/j/drl/irf/rpt/.

d. Freedom of Movement, Internally Displaced Persons, Protection of Refugees, and Stateless Persons

The constitution provides for freedom of internal movement, foreign travel, emigration, and repatriation. The government did not always respect these rights, however.

The government cooperated with the Office of the UN High Commissioner for Refugees and other humanitarian organizations in providing protection and assistance to internally displaced persons, refugees, returning refugees, asylum seekers, stateless persons, and other persons of concern.

Foreign Travel: The law provides that the government may reject for "reasonable cause" applications to obtain or renew passports, but the applicant has the right to appeal such decisions before the High Civil Court. Individuals reported that authorities banned them from travel due to unpaid debt obligations or other fiduciary responsibilities with lending institutions. Authorities relied on determinations of "national security" when adjudicating passport applications. Authorities prevented several activists from leaving the country in a few instances because they were under criminal investigation.

There were reports that authorities influenced the governments of other countries to deny entry to Bahraini citizens. In February, Dubai Airport authorities banned Mansoor al-Jamri, editor in chief of *Al-Wasat* daily, and his wife, Associated Press reporter Reem Khalifa, from entering the United Arab Emirates. In August authorities prevented Maryam al-Khawaja, BCHR acting president, from boarding a British Airlines flight to Bahrain.

Citizenship: In November 2012, citing the law, the MOI revoked the citizenship of 31 Shia Bahrainis, including two former members of parliament (brothers Jawad and Jalal Fairouz), a number of citizens and clerics of Persian descent residing in the country, and a number of ethnic Arab citizens residing abroad. Lawyers announced that the MOI confiscated the identification cards and passports of those individuals residing in the country. Ibrahim Karimi, whose citizenship was revoked, was the only affected individual who presented his case before the administrative court. The court held hearings in March, September, and October and postponed the case each time. The next hearing was scheduled for March 2014. According to press reports, the MOI summoned six of the 31 and threatened to deport Shia religious scholar Shaikh Hussain Najati if he did not depart the country.

Protection of Refugees

Access to Asylum: The law does not provide for the granting of asylum or refugee status, and the government has not established a system for providing protection to refugees. The government provided protection against the expulsion or return of refugees to countries where their lives or freedom would be threatened on account of their race, religion, nationality, membership in a particular social group, or political opinion. Such individuals generally had access to certain social services, education, and employment.

Stateless Persons

Citizenship is generally derived from the father but may be conferred or revoked by the king. Noncitizen men who marry citizen women are not entitled to citizenship, and as a result children from such marriages are not granted citizenship. The government states that children of a Bahraini woman married to a non-Bahraini man hold the nationality of the father. It was unknown how many stateless persons resided in the country. Stateless persons had access to limited social services, education, and employment. They were eligible to receive housing and other government services but excluded from receiving scholarships.

Section 3. Respect for Political Rights: The Right of Citizens to Change Their Government

Citizens do not have the right to change their government or their political system. The constitution provides for a democratically elected Council of Representatives, the lower house of parliament. A constitutional amendment ratified in May 2012 permits the king to dissolve the Council of Representatives, but it requires that he first consult the presidents of the upper and lower houses of parliament as well as the head of the Constitutional Court. The king also has the power to amend the constitution and to propose, ratify, and promulgate laws.

Elections and Political Participation

Recent Elections: The 2011 Council of Representatives by-elections were marred by irregularities. The by-elections were for the seats of 18 members from al-Wifaq who resigned in early 2011 to protest government action against demonstrators calling for political reform. Several registered political societies declined to participate and urged their supporters to boycott. Opposition political societies asserted the government gerrymandered the 40 electoral districts in 2002 to provide for a progovernment, mostly Sunni majority in the Council of Representatives. Approximately 17 percent of eligible voters participated in the two rounds of voting. The majority of the winning candidates were self-declared independents, with only two candidates claiming ties to official political societies.

Many alleged that the government engineered the victory of some female and Shia candidates by encouraging their competitors to withdraw from the race, and there were reports that some opposition political societies attempted to intimidate voters. Some candidates alleged a concerted effort by Shia election boycotters to force them to withdraw from the race.

During 2011 a number of elected municipal councils suspended several al-Wifaq political society municipal councilors because of their participation in antigovernment protests. In municipal councils where al-Wifaq members constituted a minority, Sunni members voted for their expulsion, sometimes in violation of council bylaws. In June 2012 the High Criminal Court of Appeals rejected re-instatement of five expelled municipal council members; the Court of Cassation upheld the verdict on January 21.

Political Parties: The government did not allow the formation of political parties, but more than a dozen "political societies" developed political platforms, held internal elections, and hosted political gatherings. Individuals active with opposition political society groups faced repercussions during the year. In July 2012 the government dissolved Amal, alleging it had committed "grave violations." Amal appealed the decision, and the court adjourned a session scheduled for December 31, 2012, until January. On April 15, the Court of Appeals upheld the verdict dissolving Amal.

Separately, six members of the general secretariat and four other Amal members were tried and convicted in an SNS court in 2011. In November 2012 the Higher Court of Appeals issued a verdict reducing the sentences for nine of the 10 and acquitting one. The defendants appealed their verdicts to the Court of Cassation, but no date for the hearing was set, and there was no further legal action by year's end.

Participation of Women and Minorities: Parliament's lower elected house included four women in its 40 members. The Shura Council, the appointed 40-member upper house, included 11 women. Three women served as cabinet members; there were no female judges on the criminal courts, but one sat on the Constitutional Court.

Shia and Sunni citizens have equal rights before the law, but Sunnis dominated political life, although the majority of citizens were Shia. The Shura Council included 17 Shia members, including the chairman, as well as one Jewish member. Six of the 29 cabinet ministers were Shia, including one of the four deputy prime ministers.

Section 4. Corruption and Lack of Transparency in Government

The law provides criminal penalties for official corruption, but the government did not implement the law adequately, and some officials reportedly engaged in corrupt practices with impunity. The law subjects government employees at all levels to prosecution if they use their positions to engage in embezzlement or bribery, either directly or indirectly. Penalties can be up to 10 years of imprisonment; however, no cases were brought under the law during the year.

Corruption: The Bahrain National Audit Bureau report detailed corruption, irregularities, and mismanagement in most of ministries. The report noted the government fully or partially implemented only 72 of 192 recommendations. The bureau commented that nine government ministries failed to adopt any of the recommendations cited in the 2012 report. The report also cited the Ministry of Health as a major source of corruption and irregularities and cited the Ministry of Housing and Works for cost overruns and irregularities.

In interviews with local press, the Bahrain Transparency Society stated that despite progress, concerns remained about corruption in parastatal companies. In February 2012 the former head of Aluminium Bahrain was charged in the United Kingdom with corruption and money laundering between 1999 and 2006. His trial was scheduled for 2013; no charges were filed against him in Bahrain. At a hearing on November 21, the chairman of Aluminium Bahrain claimed British lawyers attempted to intimidate him before testifying. On December 2, the media reported that British courts received documents alleging that members of the royal family played roles in signing aluminum and other business deals.

The privatization of public land continued to be a concern among opposition groups. Significant areas of government activity, including the security services and the BDF, lacked transparency. The press reported that in many cases authorities jailed or fined law enforcement and court officials for misconduct, most often for accepting bribes. The government had not announced any cases being prosecuted or investigated by year's end.

Whistleblower Protection: There was no information available on whether the law provides protection to public and private employees for making internal disclosures or lawful public disclosures of illegal action.

Financial Disclosure: The law does not require government officials to make financial disclosure statements.

Public Access to Information: The law does not provide citizens access to government-held information. Most companies and ministries have public websites, but specific budgetary information, such as individual expenditures and income, was not available. Efforts in some parts of the government to improve transparency were resisted by other officials.

Section 5. Governmental Attitude Regarding International and Nongovernmental Investigation of Alleged Violations of Human Rights

Most domestic human rights groups operated without significant government restrictions including the BHRS, the primary independent and licensed human rights organization in the country, the BCHR, which the government officially dissolved in 2004, and the unlicensed Bahrain Youth Society for Human Rights (BYSHR). The unlicensed umbrella human rights organization Bahrain Human Rights Observatory also issued numerous reports and had strong ties to international human rights NGOs. The licensed Bahrain Human Rights Watch continued to issue numerous reports and had strong ties to international NGOs.

Some domestic and international human rights groups faced difficulties operating freely. A number of international human rights representatives reported being barred from entering the country. The government maintained the five-day "working week" visa implemented in March 2012 for representatives from international human rights organizations, despite local organizations' objections that the majority of protests and incidents occurred during the weekend and the five-day visa would prevent foreign observers from accurately documenting and reporting on events.

The government arrested and harassed local NGO leaders. On May 2, authorities arrested Naji Fateel, BYSHR board member, and on May 9, the Public Prosecution charged him with "forming a group for the purpose of obstructing the provisions of the constitution," under the antiterrorism law. On May 7, the BCHR alleged that authorities tortured Fateel with electric shocks, simulated drowning, and sexual harassment while in detention at the CID. On May 16, SIU chief Nawaf Hamza reported that an SIU inspector met with Fateel in the presence of his lawyer and found no evidence of mistreatment. Fateel remained in custody, and on September 29 the High Criminal Court sentenced him to 15 years' imprisonment.

In addition to the continued detention of Nabeel Rajab and Naji Fateel, the government detained and questioned BCHR's head of documentation Sayed Yousif al-Muhafadha during the year. The government detained al-Muhafadha in December 2012 for spreading false news on Twitter, and authorities held him in custody until January when he was acquitted. In March the Public Prosecution filed for an appeal of the acquittal. On September 12, the High Criminal Court of Appeals upheld his acquittal on the charge of "spreading false information on Twitter."

A BCHR associate organization, the BYSHR, continued to operate as an unregistered NGO. In October 2012 the government detained overnight the BYSHR head, Mohammed al-Maskati, who participated in a protest in Manama. On June 19, the Lower Criminal Court adjourned al-Maskati's case, charging him with "participation in illegal protests," to July 19, September 10, and December 9. The next trial date was set for February 2014.

In 2012 the UN Human Rights Council conducted its second Universal Periodic Review (UPR) of the country's human rights situation and identified 176 recommendations for the country to implement and consider. Following the May 2012 UPR session, a number of local human rights activists, who participated in the session and criticized the government, reported local press and government officials harassed them as a result of their participation. In 2012 press reports indicated the Ministry of Interior stated that those returning from Geneva could be investigated for having slandered their country, but the government did not release further information about these investigations. At year's end the government had not publicly detailed its implementation of the UPR recommendations.

UN and Other International Bodies: The government repeatedly refused entry to representatives of international human rights organizations. The government also barred entry to representatives of foreign NGOs working to strengthen democratic institutions, civil society, and labor organizations. Brian Dooley of Human Rights First reported in March that the government denied his visa request. UN Special Rapporteur Juan Mendez' scheduled visit in May was cancelled, and authorities did not set a new date. In September, 47 countries cosponsored a joint statement on the country's human rights situation at the UN Human Rights Council session in Geneva.

Government Human Rights Bodies: In April 2012 the government established a Human Rights Ministry, distinct from the Ministry of Social Development, led by Minister Salah Ali Abdulrahman. In September 2012 the king also re-established the National Human Rights Institute as the National Human Rights Organization. According to the decree, the 15 members appointed to the organization would serve four-year terms that could be renewed once. In January the king issued a royal decree to re-establish the country's National Human Rights Organization, now recognized as the National Institution for Human Rights, to hear human rights violation complaints and investigate allegations. On February 9, the institution elected its president and vice president. The institution conducted numerous human rights workshops, seminars, and trainings, as well as prison visits and referred numerous complaints to the public prosecution office. The institution reported in December that it had registered more than 100 official complaints and received 90 requests for legal assistance. In addition it signed memorandums of understanding for cooperation with the Supreme Council for Women and the MOI Ombudsman's Office.

In 2011 the government convened the BICI, whose staff included international human rights experts, and tasked it with investigating allegations of human rights violations in February and March 2011. It presented recommendations for reform in November 2011, describing a "culture of impunity" in the security services and documenting excessive use of force, including torture and a range of other human rights violations by security forces during the unrest. On December 1, the government released an updated BICI follow-up report.

During the year the government continued making progress on BICI recommendations, including rebuilding destroyed mosques and establishing the Public Prosecution's SIU and the MOI Ombudsman's Office, as well as eliminating the law enforcement and arrest authority of the BNSA. Local and international observers continued to express concern that the government did not make significant progress on other BICI recommendations, including dropping charges against individuals engaged in nonviolent political expression, criminally charging security officers accused of abuse or torture, and integrating Shia into security forces.

Section 6. Discrimination, Societal Abuses, and Trafficking in Persons

The constitution provides for equality, equal opportunity, and the right to medical care, welfare, education, property, capital, and work for all citizens. The government protected these rights unevenly, depending on an individual's social status, sect, or gender. The law does not specifically prohibit discrimination based on race, gender, disability, language, sexual orientation and gender identity, religion, sect, or social status. The law deprives foreign workers, who made up approximately one-half of the population, of many fundamental legal, social, and economic rights.

Women

Rape and Domestic Violence: Rape is illegal. The law does not address spousal rape. Penalties for rape include life imprisonment and execution in cases where the victim is a minor younger than 16 years old or in cases where the rape leads to the victim's death. In 2012, the last year for which statistics were available, the government reported 17 cases of rape. Three of those cases were referred to the court, but there were no convictions. There were numerous reports of employers raping female domestic workers, but most victims did not seek legal redress since guilt cannot be proven in court without the testimony of witnesses to the crime.

The Migrant Workers Protection Society temporarily sheltered 132 women, including two women who reported they had been raped. The society estimated that hundreds of cases went unreported.

No government policies or laws explicitly address domestic violence. Human rights organizations alleged that spousal abuse of women was widespread. Women rarely sought legal redress for violence due to fear of social reprisal or stigma. Little public attention was devoted to the problem. The government maintained the Dar al-Aman Shelter for women and children who were victims of domestic violence. The shelter had 16 apartments with accommodations for two women in each apartment. Citizens and noncitizens were accommodated; however, a police station must refer domestic workers to the shelter. The shelter provided transportation for children to attend schools. A policewoman was stationed at the shelter, which was not identified on its exterior, to provide security.

The licensed NGO Bahrain Women's Union addressed domestic violence and held workshops to assist women seeking legal recourse for spousal abuse. During 2012, the last year for which statistics were available, the NGO recorded cases of abuse from 2011 for which women did not receive legal redress, specifically 98 cases including one case of sexual abuse and 24 cases of physical violence. In 2012 the NGO also organized a committee composed of representatives from local women's groups to review the status of family law legislation and advocate for legislative changes.

Sexual Harassment: The law prohibits sexual harassment with penalties of up to one year in prison or a fine of 100 dinars ($270) if the victim was between the ages of 14 and 21 and up to three months in prison and a fine of 20 dinars ($54) if the suspect is convicted of insulting or committing an indecent act towards a female in public. In 2012 the government stated that there were 86 cases of reported sexual harassment, 16 of which were transferred to court, five of which resulted in convictions. Although the government sometimes enforced the law, sexual harassment remained a widespread problem for women, especially foreigners employed as domestic workers and in other low-level service jobs.

Reproductive Rights: The government did not interfere with the right of couples and individuals to decide freely and responsibly the number, spacing, and timing of children and to have the information and means to do so free from discrimination, coercion, and violence. Reproductive health services, including birth control, prenatal care, essential obstetric care, and postpartum maternity care, were available without charge to all women. Health centers required women to obtain spousal consent to undergo sterilization; this consent requirement did not apply for provision of other family planning services.

Discrimination: Women faced discrimination under the law. A woman cannot transmit nationality to her spouse or children (see section 2.d., Stateless Persons). Women have the right to initiate divorce proceedings, but both Shia and Sunni religious courts may refuse the request, although the refusal rate was significantly higher in Shia courts than in Sunni courts, with Shia courts often refusing to grant the divorce due to differences in legal codes. In divorce cases the courts routinely granted mothers custody of daughters younger than age nine and sons younger than age seven. Custody usually reverted to the father once girls and boys reached the ages of nine and seven, respectively. Regardless of custody decisions, the father retains guardianship, or the right to make all legal decisions for the child, until a child reaches the age of 21. A noncitizen woman automatically loses custody of her children if she divorces their citizen father "without just cause."

Family law is based on sharia as interpreted by Sunnis and Shia. Only Sunni family law is codified, while Shia maintain separate judicial bodies composed of religious jurisprudents charged with interpreting sharia. Family law is further complicated by numerous Sunni-Shia marriages in which it is not always clear which courts have jurisdiction.

Women may own and inherit property and represent themselves in all public and legal matters. In the absence of a direct male heir, Shia women may inherit all of their husband's property, while Sunni women inherit only a portion, as governed by sharia, and the brothers or other male relatives of the deceased divide the balance. Better-educated families used wills and other legal tools to mitigate the negative effects of these rules.

Labor laws prohibit discrimination against women, but discrimination against women was systemic, especially in the workplace. Labor Law 36 (adopted in 2012) prohibits wage discrimination based on gender. Although women held positions of authority in the government and private sector, they were underrepresented. Cultural barriers and religious tradition sometimes hampered women's rights.

Children

Birth Registration: Citizenship is derived from one's father or by decree from the king. Women cannot transmit their nationality to their children, rendering stateless some children of citizen mothers but noncitizen fathers (see section 2.d., Stateless Persons). Births are not registered immediately. From birth to the age of three months, children are registered with the mother's primary health-care provider. Upon reaching three months, the birth is registered with the Ministry of Health Birth Registration Unit, which then issues the official birth certificate. Children not registered before reaching one year old must obtain a registration by court order. The government does not provide public services to a child without a birth certificate.

Education: Schooling is compulsory for children through age 14 and is provided free of charge to citizens and legal residents through grade 12. Government-run primary schools were segregated by gender, although girls and boys were educated with the same curricula and textbooks.

Child Abuse: NGOs reported an increase in child abuse cases in recent years but were unsure whether it reflected increases in abuse or greater willingness to report it. Sharia courts, not civil courts, address crimes involving child abuse, including violence against children. NGOs expressed concern over the lack of consistent written guidelines for prosecuting and punishing offenders and the leniency of penalties in child abuse cases. The Be Free Center, associated with the Bahrain Women's Association and focusing on child abuse awareness and prevention, dealt with approximately 90 cases of child abuse during the year.

On September 15, Human Rights Watch published a report entitled "Bahrain: Security Forces Detaining Children" and noted the MOI conducted between 14 and 22 "child arrests" in August and abused the children in several cases.

Forced and Early Marriage: According to the law, the minimum age of marriage is 15 years for females and 18 for males, but special circumstances allow marriages below these ages with approval from a sharia court.

Sexual Exploitation of Children: The law prohibits exploitation of a child for various crimes, including prostitution. Penalties include imprisonment of no less than three months if the accused used exploitation and force to commit the crime and up to six years if more than one child was exploited, as well as penalties of at least 2,000 dinars ($5,400) for individuals and at least 10,000 dinars ($27,000) for organizations. Penalties vary depending on the specific law involved. The law also prohibits child pornography. There is no minimum age for consensual sex, as the law assumes there is no consensual sex outside of marriage. On October 9, local media reported the Public Prosecution completed an investigation of unnamed persons accused of luring children to perform sexual acts, both as prostitutes and as subjects for internet pornography. The court ordered no other details released about this case.

International Child Abductions: The country is not a party to the 1980 Hague Convention on the Civil Aspects of International Child Abduction.

Anti-Semitism

According to community members, there were between 36 and 40 Jewish citizens (six families) in the country. Some anti-Jewish political commentary and editorial cartoons appeared in print and electronic media, usually linked to the Israeli-Palestinian conflict, without government response.

In December the ambassador to France paid an official visit to a Holocaust memorial in that country, becoming the first Arab diplomat to visit the site. His visit prompted criticism from parliamentarian Khalid al-Malood, of the al-Asala Islamic bloc, who said, "In our world today it is well known that the so-called Jewish Holocaust is just a big lie and deception just to seize Palestinian rights and lands."

Trafficking in Persons

See the Department of State's *Trafficking in Persons Report* at www.state.gov/j/tip/.

Persons with Disabilities

The law stipulates that persons with disabilities are to be treated equally with regard to employment and violations of the law are punishable with fines. The law does not address discrimination in education, air travel and other transportation, access to health care, or the provision of other state services. It was unclear whether the government enforced these laws. According to the government, a committee originally formed in 2011 to care for persons with disabilities was re-established in 2012 and included representatives from all relevant ministries, NGOs, and the private sector. The committee is responsible for monitoring violations against persons with disabilities; it was unclear whether the committee acted on any incidents during the year.

A variety of governmental, quasi-governmental, and religious institutions are mandated to support and protect persons with disabilities. New public buildings in the Central Municipality must include facilities for persons with disabilities. The law does not outline specific criteria for what is required for facilities to be accessible for persons with disabilities. The law does not mandate access to other nonresidential buildings for persons with disabilities. There was no information available regarding a law providing access for persons with disabilities to information and communication.

There were no official reports of discrimination against persons with disabilities in employment, education, or access to health care. There was no information available on the responsibilities of government agencies to protect the rights of persons with disabilities and actions taken by government agencies to improve respect for their rights. According to anecdotal evidence, however, such persons routinely lacked access to education and employment. The one government school for children with hearing disabilities did not operate past the 10th grade. Some public schools had specialized education programs for children with learning disabilities, physical handicaps, speech impediments, and Down syndrome, but the government did not fund private programs for children who could not find appropriate programs in public schools.

The law requires the government to provide vocational training for persons with disabilities who wish to work. The law also requires employers of more than 100 persons to hire at least 2 percent of its employees from the government's list of workers with disabilities. The government did not monitor compliance. The government placed persons with disabilities in some public sector jobs.

On September 18, Minister of Social Development and Chairperson for the High Committee for Persons with Disabilities Fatima Mohammed al-Balooshi announced the launch of a National Strategy for the Rights of Persons with Disabilities. Al-Balooshi stated that the national strategy is based on human rights and focuses on the principles embedded in the UN Charter and the Convention on the Rights of Persons with Disabilities. She further noted that the strategy was formed in cooperation with the UN Development Program and based on seven main themes: legislation, health and rehabilitation, education, economic and social empowerment, economic empowerment of women with disabilities, easy access to buildings and services and information, and awareness.

National/Racial/Ethnic Minorities

The law grants citizenship to Arab applicants who have resided in the country for 15 years and non-Arab applicants who have resided in the country for 25 years. There was a lack of transparency in the naturalization process, and there were numerous reports that the citizenship law was not applied uniformly. There were allegations that the government allowed foreign Sunni employees of the security services who had lived in the country for fewer than 15 years to apply for citizenship. There were also reports that Arab Shia who had resided in the country for more than 15 years and non-Arab foreign residents who had resided more than 25 years had not been granted citizenship. There were reports of general discrimination, especially in employment practices, against Shia citizens of Persian ethnicity (Ajam).

Foreign citizens continued to operate the Federation of Expat Associations with a stated goal to facilitate cooperation among civil societies for foreign citizens to promote common interests.

Although the government asserted that the labor code for the private sector applies to all workers, the International Labor Organization (ILO) and international NGOs noted that foreign workers faced discrimination in the workplace (see section 7).

There were reports of South Asians being attacked during the year. On March 17, a Bangladeshi man was seriously injured after he touched a homemade explosive in al-Dair village. On June 9, an Asian man suffered severe burns when he was attacked with Molotov cocktails. According to testimony provided to the BICI, the attackers targeted the individuals due to their ethnicity.

Societal Abuses, Discrimination, and Acts of Violence Based on Sexual Orientation and Gender Identity

The law does not criminalize same-sex sexual activity between consenting persons who are at least 21 years of age, but there were reported cases of individuals punished for same-sex sexual activity. Lesbian, gay, bisexual, and transgender (LGBT) activities such as same-sex relationships and same-sex sexual activity were not socially accepted, and discrimination based on sexual orientation or gender identity was common. There were no open manifestations of LGBT activity in the country, such as gay pride parades.

In April a judge sentenced two Chinese migrant workers who pleaded guilty to prostitution and homosexual conduct to five years' imprisonment followed by deportation. The press quoted the judge as saying the sentence would serve as a deterrent to others and "homosexuality ruins individuals and nations."

Other Societal Violence or Discrimination

The media reported few cases of HIV/AIDS. There were no known reports of societal violence or discrimination against persons based on HIV/AIDS status, but medical experts acknowledged publicly that discrimination existed. The government mandated screening of newly arrived migrant workers for infectious diseases, including HIV/AIDS. Migrant workers found to be HIV-positive were at times deported in the past, but the status of deportations during the year was unclear.

At year's end there was no further information on implementation of the national social and economic reconciliation plan (Wi'da Wa'da).

The December BICI follow-up report noted that the Ministry of Education continued to work with UNESCO experts on incorporating human rights principles in textbooks. The report also indicated that the ministry had signed cooperation agreements with the International Bureau of Education in Geneva.

Section 7. Worker Rights

a. Freedom of Association and the Right to Collective Bargaining

The constitution and labor code recognize the right to form independent trade unions and the right to strike, with significant restrictions. The law does not provide for the right to collective bargaining.

The law prohibits trade unions in the public sector. Public sector workers may join private sector trade unions and professional associations, although these entities cannot bargain on their behalf. Members of the military services also are prohibited from joining unions. Foreign workers, who made up approximately 60 percent of the workforce, may join unions, although they typically do not play leadership roles. The law prohibits unions from engaging in political activities and requires all trade unions to affiliate with one of the country's two legal federations, the General Federation of Bahrain Trade Unions (GFBTU) or the Bahrain Free Labor Union Federation. The law excludes domestic workers from these limited permissions.

The law specifies that only a trade union can organize and declare legal strikes and imposes excessive requirements for legal strikes. The law prohibits strikes in 10 "vital" sectors--the scope of which exceeds international standards--including the oil, gas, education, telecommunications, transportation, and health sectors, as well as in pharmacies and bakeries. Workers must approve a strike with a simple majority by secret ballot and provide 15 days' notification to the employer before conducting a strike.

Law 35, passed in March 2012, significantly amended the labor code as it pertains to trade unions and federations. The law allows multiple trade union federations but prohibits multisectoral labor federations and bars individuals convicted of violating criminal laws leading to trade union or executive council dissolution from holding union leadership posts. The amendment gives the minister of labor, rather than the unions, the right to select the federation to represent workers in national-level bargaining and international forums. The law does not prohibit antiunion discrimination, nor does it require re-instatement of workers fired for union activity.

Freedom of association was generally not respected. Relations between the main federations and the Ministry of Labor were publicly contentious at times. The government sometimes interfered in GFBTU activities. For example, in October 2012 several international labor leaders and representatives from the ILO were denied entry to the country after being invited to attend the GFBTU's annual congress. The GFBTU also alleged the legal amendments allowing the minister of labor to select a representative union were intended to undermine its position as the country's representative labor federation. In May, however, the ministry again designated the GFBTU as the country's representative, subject to review every six months.

Following a revision to the law, which provided for multiple trade union federations, a second federation, the Bahrain Free Labor Unions Federation, was established in July 2012. Some workers and union affiliates complained that union pluralism had resulted in company management choosing to negotiate with the union that they found most favorable to the detriment of existing collective bargaining agreements and the legitimate voice of workers. The revised law also grants the minister of labor full discretion to designate which federation would represent workers before national and international fora rather than workers' organizations.

During the year the government made efforts to ensure the re-instatement of workers dismissed or suspended during the 2011 State of National Safety. It continued working with the tripartite committee, formed in 2011 and consisting of a representative from the Ministry of Labor, the Bahrain Chamber of Commerce and Industry, and the GFBTU, to address dismissals and re-instatements as part of the government's response to recommendations set forth in the 2011 BICI. In November the ILO visited the country to facilitate a tripartite agreement. The ministry postponed signing the agreement pending a "legal review."

Disagreement over the number of workers dismissed or re-instated continued throughout the year. The GFBTU defined a case as resolved only when the employee returned to the same position; the government considered the case resolved when an employee returned to work, regardless of the position. By the end of 2012, the government asserted 100 percent of cases in the public sector had been resolved and fewer than 1 percent of private sector cases remained unresolved and subject to litigation. The GFBTU maintained that several hundred cases remained unresolved; however, they were unable to provide thorough documentation of those claims.

In addition to some workers not being re-instated to their same or equivalent positions, some re-instated workers alleged that some companies insisted they sign loyalty pledges and agreements not to strike, despite such requirements being illegal. Groups of workers continued to protest at the Ministry of Labor and elsewhere to demand re-instatement to their original positions. Workers reported many cases of discrimination in hiring and promotion, including in the public sector. Some civil service employees, including in the Ministry of Education, reported being questioned about their outside activities.

In July the Labor Ministry held talks with foreign government representatives under the aegis of an existing free trade agreement. Both sides agreed to continue working to address outstanding issues.

b. Prohibition of Forced or Compulsory Labor

The law prohibits all forms of forced or compulsory labor except in national emergencies, but the government did not effectively enforce the law. There were reports of forced labor in the construction and service sectors. Foreign workers are covered by labor laws, but enforcement was lax, and cases of debt bondage were common. There were also reports that forced labor practices occurred among domestic workers and others working in the informal sector, most of whom are not protected by labor laws. In July 2012 the government amended the labor law to provide domestic workers the right to see their terms of employment. The government did not undertake specific efforts to enforce laws against forced labor.

In many cases employers withheld passports, restricted movement, substituted contracts, or did not pay wages; some employers also threatened workers and subjected them to physical and sexual abuse. The Ministry of Labor reported 256 complaints from domestic workers, mostly of unpaid wages. No updated information was available on the case of five Ghanaian women reportedly stranded and imprisoned in the country by their employer.

Estimates of the proportion of migrant workers in the country under illegal "free visa" arrangements--a practice that can contribute to debt bondage--ranged from 10 to 25 percent. In numerous cases employers withheld salaries from foreign workers for months or years and refused to grant them permission to leave the country. The fear of deportation or employer retaliation prevented many foreign workers from complaining to authorities.

c. Prohibition of Child Labor and Minimum Age for Employment

The minimum age for employment is 15 years, and the minimum age for hazardous work is 18. Children under 18 may not work in industries that the Ministry of Health deemed hazardous or unhealthy, including construction, mining, and oil refining. Minors under the age of 18 may work no more than six hours a day--no more than four consecutively--and may be present on the employment premises no more than seven hours a day. The Ministry of Labor made rare exceptions on a case-by-case basis for juveniles between the ages of 14 and 15 who had an urgent need to assist in providing financial support for their families. Child labor regulations do not apply to family-operated businesses in which the only other employees are family members.

Labor Law 36, which went into effect in December 2012, requires that before the Ministry of Labor makes a final decision on allowing a minor to work, the prospective employer must present documentation from the minor's guardian giving the minor permission to work, proof that the minor underwent a physical fitness examination to confirm suitability, and assurance from the employer that the minor will not be working in an environment that the ministry has deemed hazardous. In general the government effectively enforced the law.

Some non-Bahraini children were employed as domestic servants. Some Bahraini children were believed to work in family-run businesses, but the practice did not appear widespread.

According to NGOs, government labor inspectors monitored and enforced child labor laws effectively in the industrial sector.

Also see the Department of Labor's *Findings on the Worst Forms of Child Labor* at www.dol.gov/ilab/programs/ocft/tda.htm.

d. Acceptable Conditions of Work

There is no national private sector minimum wage. A standardized government pay scale covers public sector workers, with a set minimum of 300 dinars ($810) per month. Citizens who earned less received a government stipend to offset the difference. There is no minimum wage for foreign workers in the public sector, although the government issued "guidelines" advising employers in the public and private sectors to pay a minimum of 150 dinars per month ($405). There was no official poverty level.

Subject to the provisions of the new private sector law, a worker may not be employed for more than 48 hours per week. Muslim workers may not be employed during the month of Ramadan for more than six hours per day, or 36 hours per week. The standard workday is eight hours, with a maximum of 10 hours worked. Overtime rates are time-and-a-quarter during the day and time-and-a-half during the evening. It is mandatory for workers to be given 24 consecutive hours off per week, and the day set for weekly rest is Friday. If a worker is required to work on a mandatory rest day, the worker will be paid at time-and-a-half. A worker may not work on mandatory rest days for two consecutive weeks without personal written consent.

The Ministry of Labor sets occupational safety and health standards. The labor law and relevant protections apply to citizens and noncitizens alike, with the exception of domestic workers. Labor Law 36 improved the legal situation for many workers as it pertains to access to contracts and additional holidays, although it exempts domestic workers from the majority of protections.

The Labor Ministry is responsible for enforcing the labor law and mandating acceptable conditions of work. During the year the ministry employed 24 labor inspectors, and the Labor Market Regulatory Authority reportedly employed 48 inspectors. The ministry enforced occupational safety and health standards; it also used a team of six engineers from multiple specialties primarily to investigate risks and standards at construction sites, which made up the vast majority of worksites.

Inspections were triggered by a complaint made to the ministry, notification of a new worksite made to the ministry, a news article about a new worksite, or when an inspector discovered a new worksite in an assigned geographic area.

Inspectors have the authority to levy fines and close worksites if employers do not improve conditions by specified deadlines. Penalties for violators range from 500 dinars ($1,350) to 1,000 dinars ($2,700) per violation or per worker affected, or both, as determined by a judge. Additionally, a judge may also sentence violators to a minimum of three months in prison. For repeat violators the penalties may be doubled. The ministry reported an unspecified number of violators were serving sentences related to labor condition violations during the year.

Despite the improvements NGOs feared that resources for enforcement of the laws remained inadequate for the number of worksites and workers, that many worksites would not be inspected, and that the regulations would not necessarily deter violations.

A ministerial decree prohibits outdoor work between noon and 4 p.m. during July and August. The ban was enforced among large firms, but according to local sources, violations were common among smaller businesses. After inspecting 24,036 work sites, the Ministry of Labor reported that 99 percent of inspected companies were in compliance with the summer outdoor work ban during the year, significantly increased from 2007 when only 85 percent of companies were in compliance.

The government and the courts generally worked to rectify abuses brought to their attention. Workers could lodge complaints with the Labor Ministry. The ministry reported that it received 2,121 complaints, including joint complaints, brought during the year by 856 female and 1,265 male workers. Labor officials stated they were able to resolve most cases through mediation. The ministry stated these complaints resulted in 144 violations sent to the public prosecutor. By law complaints that cannot be settled through arbitration must be referred to the court within 15 days. The vast majority of cases involving abused domestic workers did not reach the ministry or the public prosecutor.

During 2012 inspectors visited 821 labor camps to verify that workers' accommodations met required safety and hygiene standards. They reported violations in 328 of the 821 camps and issued final warnings to 80 establishments, written warnings to 172, and verbal warnings to 159. No violations were found in 82 establishments.

Limited access to private homes and the limited number of inspectors impeded full enforcement of standards, particularly in the informal sector and among domestic servants. Regulations authorize labor officials to inspect only premises that have a commercial registration; they may not inspect private homes, where most domestic workers lived and worked, or unregistered "private" camps, where many unskilled foreign laborers lived and where conditions were the worst. The Labor Ministry advised the Ministry of Municipalities and the Ministry of Housing when it received complaints of poor conditions in such housing.

The government continued to conduct workers' rights awareness campaigns. It published pamphlets on foreign resident workers' rights in several languages, provided manuals on these rights to local diplomatic missions, and operated a telephone hotline for victims. Additionally, the Ministry of Labor held several meetings in conjunction with relevant diplomatic missions to bring together workers to discuss issues in their native languages and provide materials that explained their rights in both the formal and informal economies. No new information was available at the end of the year.

Violations of wage, overtime, and occupational safety and health standards were common in sectors employing foreign migrant workers, such as construction, automotive repair, and domestic service. Unskilled foreign workers, mostly from South and Southeast Asia, were approximately 60 percent of the total workforce (76 percent of the private sector workforce). These workers were also vulnerable to dangerous or exploitive working conditions. According to NGOs workplace safety inspection and compliance were substandard.

A 2009 study by the governmental Labor Market Regulatory Authority found that 65 percent of foreign workers had not seen their employment contract and 89 percent were unaware of their terms of employment. While the study was not renewed, local sources confirmed lack of awareness on terms of employment remained a problem. Some foreign workers arrived in the country under the sponsorship of an employer and then switched jobs while continuing to pay a fee to their original sponsor, which made it difficult to monitor and control their employment. Some employers illegally charged workers exorbitant fees to remain in the country and work for other employers.

The labor law does not fully protect domestic workers, and this group was particularly vulnerable to exploitation. In July 2012 the government amended the labor law to expand the rights of domestic employees, who had not been covered under the previous law. Labor Law 36 requires domestic employees to be employed under "clear contractual terms" and provides for penalties for violators. The amendments, however, do not accord domestic employees all of the rights that Law 36 provides to other private sector workers, including limits on daily and weekly working hours and weekly days off.

There were credible reports that many of the country's 70,000 domestic workers, most of them women, were forced to work 12- to 16-hour days, had to give their identity documents to employers, had little time off, were malnourished, and were subject to verbal and physical abuse, including sexual molestation and rape. Reports of employers and recruitment agents beating or sexually abusing foreign women working in domestic positions were common. Numerous instances were reported in the press and to embassies and police. During the year the Ministry of Labor reported it received 256 complaints from domestic workers, a sharp rise from 2012. The ministry reported that most complaints were related to employer's failure to pay salaries, and it took unspecified action to compel employers to pay the suspended salaries.

The vast majority of cases involving abused domestic workers did not reach the Ministry of Labor or the public prosecutor for a variety of reasons. Most victims were too intimidated to sue their employers, although they had the right to do so. NGOs also reported that the court system made it difficult for workers, who frequently did not have home addresses, to receive notices about their cases once they filed them. Although victims may assign power of attorney to someone in the country to permit the victim to return home, most did not use this option due to financial constraints prohibiting employees from working for a new sponsor until the case with the previous sponsor is resolved.

During the year the Migrant Workers Protection Society shelter provided more than 100 female domestic workers with temporary housing and assistance with their cases. The majority of women in these cases sought assistance with unpaid wages and complaints of physical abuse. The Migrant Workers Protection Society continued to support victims who took their cases to court, but by law victims can receive only outstanding unpaid wages--no criminal damages are possible unless the victim has alleged a crime found in the criminal penal code, such as physical abuse or rape. NGOs confirmed that while some cases were successful, compensation was meager.

The media reported at least 25 workers died in workplace accidents during the year. The deaths were due to a combination of inadequate enforcement of standards, blatant violations of standards, inadequate safety procedures, worker ignorance of those procedures, and inadequate safety standards for equipment. According to NGO sources, most accidents were in the construction sector, which employed more Bangladeshis and Pakistanis than other nationalities. In October a Bangladeshi man fell to his death from a second-floor construction site; the Ministry of Labor confirmed he was an illegal worker and stated the employer would be fined 1,000 dinars ($2,700) "for violations." In November a Bangladeshi worker fell to his death when a rope snapped. The man reportedly was not wearing safety equipment.

In October local media reported a suicide attempt by an Indonesian migrant worker, noting 24 similar attempts by expatriate workers during the year. The Migrant Workers Protection Society noted that suicide attempts were common among Indian workers and were underreported in the media.

Conditions in the many unregistered or illegal worker camps were often poor. Safety of accommodations and quality of life for workers were problems that continued to be a major concern at source country embassies.